Bunkie

VIOLET BROOKE

authorHOUSE®

AuthorHouse™
1663 Liberty Drive
Bloomington, IN 47403
www.authorhouse.com
Phone: 1 (800) 839-8640

Published by AuthorHouse   04/17/2015

ISBN: 978-1-5049-0431-5 (sc)
ISBN: 978-1-5049-0432-2 (hc)
ISBN: 978-1-5049-0430-8 (e)

Library of Congress Control Number: 2015904949

Print information available on the last page.

DEDICATION

I would like to dedicate this book to my mom and dad because they were always there for us. They gave to us in their own way, which was not easy for them at all. We survived and had a good life.

Mama was a kind and hard working woman. She didn't know how to show love because there was no one to show her.

Daddy always watched out for us in his own way. He always allowed me to do anything I wanted, but he shared in nothing I did.

I have a wonderful husband of fifty-five years, who has devoted his whole life to me, our three girls, and their families. No one could ever be so kind, loving, and caring as his is to all of us. God has blessed us.

I want to thank God, my husband John, my three daughters: Susan, Bonny, and Melinda, for making my life so special.

My granddaughter, Bobby Lynn Graves, helped me put this book together and I thank her for all of her help.

This is the true story of my life...

Hi. My name is Bunkie. I was born on a farm in 1935, to poor, but strict parents. We were all born at home with the help of Dr. Snead. I am sure that mother didn't have an easy time of it. The old colored woman from back in the woods came to wash clothes and cook for us. I was the fifth child. My older sisters were grown when I first knew them. I forgot to tell you that we were all girls, eight of us.

When I was five years old, I came to know who I was. Walter Duzla gave me my name. I remember him coming in his truck to help us on the farm. During the depression, Mom and Dad lost everything. They lost the car, the truck, and everything else they had. Walter would come to carry calves, pigs, potatoes, and whatever else could be taken to market. He was a nice man. The Tokarz family lived nearby and we were not allowed to have anything to do with them. I thought they were nice people, although I couldn't understand them. They were Polish. We lived way back in the woods, a mile and a half away from the main road. Other than my grandmother, two uncles, the Tokarz family, and Walter Duzla, I never saw anyone else.

We had pigs, chickens, cows, horses, cats, and an old dog. There was always a lot to do on the farm. The hens had to be fed and watered. The eggs would be gathered up and their nests would be cleaned. The horses had to be watered and fed. The cows milked and the stable cleaned. The wood had to be chopped and brought in. The corn shucked for the hens and horses; the shucks put in for the cows. Hay was placed in the mangers for the horses, while the hogs and pigs were fed and watered.

I loved being outside. I would watch my Dad milking the cows. Every time I watched he would squirt milk in my face. I wanted to learn how to milk the cows, so my father taught me how when I was five years old.

Sometimes the old cow didn't like what I was doing and she would kick me hard. Even though it hurt, I always hung in there. After we were finished milking they had to be taken out to a field. Chains would go around their horns; we had to carry an ax and stake to drive into the ground. The cows would be tied in the field all day. Sometimes they would run away and we could not hold them back. One old cow was really mean. She saw my little sister and ran over her twice before I could get the cow away from her. My little sister was bruised, but was okay. We didn't go to the doctor for anything so we had to be tough.

Allow me to return to the time when I was five, so I can tell you a little about what happened. My two older sisters were married. The oldest one married a man that was as big as a giant and could eat as much. They had a car and would come to see us at Thanksgiving and Christmas. I was glad he didn't come more often because I would be skinny. He would sit at the table and eat a whole forty pound turkey by himself.

Although he had an appetite, he was kind. One Christmas he helped Mom and Dad put in kitchen cabinets. We had a very poor house to live in. The kitchen had a woodstove, an old wooden table and benches with a sideboard which kept flour, lard, and sour milk. There was a washstand with a basin and bucket of water for drinking. Those few things were all the contents of our kitchen. Our bedroom had two iron beds, a dresser with two drawers, and an old sewing machine stacked with washed feed bags to make our clothes. Our family room had two worn chairs, a well-used sofa, and an old woodstove to help keep the house warm.

In Mom and Dad's room there was an iron bed, a wardrobe, and a dressing table. There was also the baby's bed, which was made of wood. It had four legs and the sides were made of screen wire, the top was covered with a curtain to keep out the flies and the mosquitoes. There were no screens on the windows or the doors, so mosquitoes and flies were unrelenting. Roaches were also bad, they were everywhere at night. On Saturdays, the kitchen table and benches were turned over and hot water was poured on them, the floor would be covered with bugs. We were used to them, along with the mice and the occasional blacksnake.

I was never afraid of any of the bugs, mice, or snakes. The only thing that I was scared of was the boggie-man. Mother always said that if you don't behave the boggie-man will get you. I didn't know where he was or who he was or what he would do to me, so I always tried to be good. I tried even though I liked to fight with my younger and older sisters. They would beat up on me, too.

One day my younger sister and I were playing hide and seek. I ran into the cow stable and climbed up on the manger. Then I jumped down on a stack of rusty nails, driving one right into the center of my knee. I couldn't cry, but I had to do something. I gritted my teeth and pulled hard, out came the nail. It hurt, but I continued to play for a few more minutes. Then, I went into the house and climbed into bed. This was early in June and by mid-June I was finally myself again but I could not walk. Daddy went into the woods and cut a small tree to make me a crutch. With my crutch, I was able to go outside again and happy. In two months, I was able to walk again, but not run. My knee would really hurt if I did too much.

The summer went by and Mom was busy sewing the feedbags for our clothes. She would make us two dresses, two pairs of underwear, and a slip for the year. We would each get a pair of shoes and two pairs of socks. It was time for me to go to school. My other sister told me that I needed to learn to write my name. So we went out to the road, where there was smooth sand

and we leveled it off. She took a stick and wrote my name into the sand: Violet Lee Moore. I said, "Peter that is not my name." (My sister's name was Mary but we always called her Peter). I continued, "My name is Bunkie." Peter said, "Not anymore, you have to learn how to write and spell your name." It was in this way that I got a new name. We all had nicknames and our daddy didn't know our real names. Our names were (oldest to youngest) Horse, Click, Dick, Peter, Bunkie, Duggie, Frog, and Dukie. My sisters and I were so different from each other. I practiced writing my name in the sand until I knew it. Peter said to me, "Now you are not so dumb, at least you know your name."

We had strict rules about our clothing. You had to wear the same clothes for a week, and then you could put on clean ones for the next week. Your shoes had to come off during the first part of May and would be put away until the first of October. During this time, we went barefoot. Our feet became tough and when you finally put shoes back on you would get blisters on your heels. They would get very sore sometimes.

September came and school was about to start. I didn't want to go because I had never been away before. I had never seen more houses or people. I had never seen a town or a school before. We all got up early, dressed, and began the long walk to meet the bus. I forgot to tell you that our house had no bathrooms, running water, electricity, refrigerator, radio, TV, newspapers, telephone. We had three things, however, oxtcan soap, a Sears & Roebuck catalog, and baking soda. We had no toothbrushes, so we would wet our fingers and put baking soda on them to brush our teeth. The oxtcan soap was used to wash ourselves, the dishes and clothes. The Sears & Roebuck catalog was kept in the outhouse for special times; what a blessing it was.

We walked down the muddy lane, passing all of the mud holes and came to the shed of Moss Sherman. He was a mean old man. If it was raining, he wouldn't let us stand in the shed. He would make us stand out in the rain. As soon as he left, we would stand in the shed until the school bus came. Peter and I got onto the bus, where there were more boys and girls. I had never seen a boy before, and they look so different from me. They began to laugh at me because I had such little hair for a girl. After giving them a mean look they stopped. I was a little scared because I didn't know where the boggie-man was. At home, I knew that I was safe, but on the bus I wasn't sure.

Mr. Taylor was the bus driver's name. He was a kind man. We made more stops and more children got onto the bus until the bus was fully loaded. When we finally got to school, Peter said, "Your classroom is around the back of the school." As I walked around the corner to go to my classroom, an ugly girl knocked me down, tore my dress, gave me a black eye, and split my lip before I was even knew what was happening. Why she did this, I didn't know; I had never even seen this girl before. The teacher gave me a safety pin to pin up my dress in the front and cleaned me up some. She was nice. The rest of the day, I had the sniffles. All I could think about was that girl and how to get even with her. She made me angry and I didn't know what to do.

When I went home, my mother was mad at me for fighting on the first day of school and getting my new dress torn. All I had in mind was what to do. I had to get tough. Really tough. I knew exactly what to do. I would find her first and beat the stuffing out of her before she knew what was happening. The next day I got up early, ate my 10 biscuits and eggs. I felt good, I felt tough.

The bus came and we went to school. I crept around the opposite side of the school building and saw her standing there waiting for me. I snuck up behind her and beat her up good. She never bothered me again. I felt tough and no one ever bothered me again.

At school, we had no cafeteria. For lunch Mom made me watermelon preserves on a biscuit, which the ants liked so much, there was no lunch left to eat. We had one boy in the class who liked to eat everyone else's lunch at recess. Another boy decided to get even with him, so he brought a block of chocolate exlax and placed it in his lunch box. The next day his lunch was gone along with the exlax chocolate. Afterwards, we heard that the boy who ate the chocolate was in the hospital and not doing well. He never fully recovered. This made me very sad.

The fall had gone and Christmas was coming. It was time to find cedar trees. Peter and I took the axe to find one. We found one in the fence row down back of the barn. We nailed a board to the bottom of the cedar tree and put in the corner of the living room. It was a big tree and took up a lot of the room. We made rings out of paper and took flour and water to make paste. We found pine cones and birds nests for our tree. We popped popcorn and made a string of it to put on the tree. It looked very Christmas-y. Mama had a few Christmas balls to add to it. Daddy bought a turkey and we had ham from the smoke house. Santa Claus was coming. How exciting it was! We couldn't sleep.

The next morning we all had an apple, an orange, and whole bucket of hard candy. It was delicious. We ate candy and ate candy until the whole bucket was just about gone. It snowed the night before and the snow was about fifteen inches deep. As the evening progressed we saw three people come up from the Tokarz place. There were two boys and a young man. They were bringing a gift for my other sister. It was getting dark and Mama lit the oil lamp. They were the Dean boys and he brought my sister a box which had a mirror, a brush, and comb. When they opened up the box, one of the boys was so nervous that he hit the lamp and set the curtains on fire. Daddy took the curtains off of the window and put out the fire. Before we knew what was happening, those three boys were running home as fast as they could. The fire made me scared, but everything was fine now.

It was time to go to school again. Everyone was so excited about what they got for

Christmas. The teacher called on each of us to tell the class what Santa brought us. I told the class that I got so many things, that I couldn't remember them all.

It was recess at school. It was a big recess, which meant that we had a half-hour to do whatever we wanted to do. Janet and Juniata talked me into going to the drugstore with them. I had never been to a store before. There were things there I had never seen before. Candy of all kinds, cookies of every color; you name it and it was there. Janet came over to me and said, "Take what you want, we do it all the time." I protested that I didn't have any money.

She said, "You don't need money, we just take what we want...I will cover for you." I knew it was stealing but I took a candy bar. After I left the store, I knew I had done a bad thing. This I kept to myself, I couldn't ever go back to that store though. If Mom and Dad knew what I had done——I didn't even want to think about it.

The winter was cold——the house was cold. The bucket of water was frozen every morning. The long walk to the bus stop would make my bad knee freeze up. I had to squat down and get it warm before I could walk any further. My sister told me that my birthday was in January. We never celebrated birthdays. At school, the teacher asked me what I got for my birthday. Not knowing what to say, I told her I got so many things. That was the end of that.

Easter came and we colored hen eggs. We brought six to school for an Easter egg hunt. The next day Mrs. Moody invited us all over to her house for the hunt. They had a beautiful brick home with electricity, phone, bathroom, great furniture, the yard was cut and there were tulips blooming. Rosser Moody was in my grade and this was his home. He even had a bedroom of his own. How lucky can one person be? He didn't have to work the long rows in the fields.

He had a bicycle to ride, a store to go to, candy and soda pop whenever he wanted it. I bet he never wanted for anything. Here we were at an Easter egg hunt; me in my feedbag dresses and him with all of this. It made me feel sad. Why didn't I have all of this?

Spring was coming soon. One of our horses died, so my sister's husband talked Daddy into buying a tractor. He said that he knew a man in Gloucester who had an A-Farmall and it had a cultivator, plow, and disk with it. He wanted $125.00 for it. Daddy went to the bank and borrowed the money. In a few days, Walter Duzla brought the tractor and equipment to us. A real tractor, I thought. I wanted to learn how to drive it.

Daddy was busy getting the land ready to plant potatoes. Every year he would put aside thirty bushels to use as seed potatoes. Mr. Getty had a potato house in Toano and he would let him keep them there. I was 7 now, strong and tough, I wanted to help. We had an old potato planter but it was pulled by big horses. Daddy had to cut the tongue off of it and put a hitch to fit the bar on the tractor. That worked quite well. In the second week of March it was time to cut potatoes. Thirty bushels was a lot of potatoes. The potatoes were brought into the kitchen and we learned how to cut them, so that each one would have an eye. That is where the new plants would come from, the eyes. They had to be cut seven to ten days before planting.

Once the land was ready, one person had to work the potato planter while another one drove the tractor. Instead of going to school, I got to drive the tractor. I was happy that I could drive and drive all day long. At night I was so tired. Three days later I went back to school. The teacher wanted to know where I had been, so I told her about driving the tractor. They all laughed at me; because they knew that I couldn't drive anything.

Easter came and that year my sister's husband came from Newport News to see us. He told dad that he could buy a used army truck for $75.00 and that he could get it for him. We bought the truck for the farm. We had a tractor and an army truck. The next week it arrived--big, brown, and ugly. I was excited because I could drive this now. I watched how to drive it, and in no time I could drive it all by myself.

The army truck broke down. It always had flat tires every time we got it loaded. So my sister's husband, the giant, said that he would fix it if we brought it to his house in Newport News. On Saturday we drove it down to their house. This was the end of July and the watermelons were just getting ripe. Daddy picked about five of them to bring to my sister. We arrived at their house at noon, just in time for dinner. I was hungry and so was Daddy. It was hot that day so we brought the watermelons into the house.

The kitchen in my sister's house was so small that you could barely turn around in it. Daddy sat the watermelons on the floor and stood up. My sister had left a cabinet door open and when he rose up, he hit his head on the edge of the cabinet door, sending blood flying. It almost knocked him out. There he sat on the floor with the two watermelons. My sister got a wet towel and pressed it to his bald head. The blood finally stopped, but Daddy wasn't right the rest of the day.

Maynard started to work on the truck at about 2 o'clock. He worked and worked, at midnight he said it was all fixed. So we started home at 12:30. He put on a new water pump and head gasket; of course, he forgot to put water in the radiator. We got about a mile away from their house and the truck started to smoke. We stopped and raised up the hood. Seeing that the radiator was dry, we found some water and put it in real slow, so it wouldn't bust the head. At about 1:30 we were finally on our way home again.

Morning was coming and it was time to milk the cows and feed the animals. I knew Daddy's head was still hurting. He went to get some hay off of the platform for the cows. He jumped off the platform, sticking the pitchfork right through the top of his foot. Boy, did he let out a howl. We pulled it out and Mama soaked it in hot salt water. Then she went to the smoke house and cut two pieces of fat-back to put on it. One piece on top and one piece on the bottom. In about a week it was well, but sore.

The summer turned hot and dry. The watermelon and sweet potatoes did well; saving us financially. Mama found out that she is having another baby, an eighth child to be exact. Daddy bought a new truck because the Army Truck stayed broken down or had flat tires.

We planted corn, potatoes, sweet potatoes, hay, watermelon, turnips, salad, and cabbage that year. School was out and Daddy cut the hay with the tractor and mower, but the hay had to be raked by the horse drawn hay rake. It was hot and the middle of the day, so I asked Daddy if I could rake the hay while they got it up with the tractor and wagon.

He thought about it and asked if I was sure I could do it. "Sure," I said, confident in my abilities.

He hitched the old horse up and I climbed onto the rake's seat. My feet were just able to push the trip lever to let the hay come out in a roll. Up the road we went. When we arrived at the field, the horse and I made several rounds around the field and the hay was raking fine. On the third round, we were coming up on the woods again. All of a sudden, four wild dogs came out of the woods at the horse, growling at her. The horse took off like a scared rabbit, throwing me between her tail and the bars. The hay rake was flying up and down like crazy. I still had the reins in my hands and I tried to get up, but was unsuccessful. I started talking to the horse, saying "Whoa, Whoa girl." Finally she stopped and I was able to get off of the bars and stand up. Walking in front of the horse, I led her home and told Daddy what happened. He finished raking the hay and I went to bed. Sore for a week, I never tried raking hay again.

August had come and it was time to shuck the corn. Taking eight rows at a time, every fifteen feet you would tie six corn stalks together. Then we took a corn knife and cut the corn off at the bottom of the stalks and stacking it against the tied off corn stalks. Cutting twelve rows at a time was called pile row. After it was cut and staked we had a rope and pulley, we wrapped around the middle of each pile and pulled it tight. Next we would tie it with binder twine. It was left to dry in the field. In the fall we would take the corn shucks to the barn to be shucked out for the animals. This would be feed for all the chickens, pigs, cows and horses.

This particular August, something different happened. During World War II, there was a German prison camp in Newport News. A truck showed up and out of the cab came two big men with shot guns. In the back of the truck were five men, all dressed alike. Daddy made us go to the house. They got out and started to cut corn. They cut all day just for a meal. They could really shock corn, but they never came back. This was a strange event, but a big help.

Mother was about to have another baby and it was time to start school again. If the days were good we stayed home to dig sweet potatoes. My younger sister was six years old and big enough to work. But when the baby was born, Peter wanted to take care of it. She loved to be in the house and take care of babies. She hated outside and Mama let her stay in. We had ten acres of sweet potatoes to dig by hand. I would get up early if I was going to school and help him plow out a pile-row, which was five rows turned one way and five turned the other. This left a nice clean place to throw the potatoes in piles every eight feet apart, so they could be packed according to size. We had a bushel basket which some of the potatoes were packed for shipping the next day. The crop turned out particularly well that year and we finally had some extra money.

Dad heard that the Tokarz family was going to sell their place. He went to see them and bought the farm for $500.00. This meant more land to farm, which was exciting. With

Daddy driving the tractor during the day and hauling our produce to the market, we were doing well.

I was now going on 7 ½ years old and my younger sister was getting ready to go to school that year. I knew I would have to watch out for her, so that girl wouldn't beat up on her. My classroom this year was in the big school building. It was nice, but I had never seen a toilet stool before. There were five of them and a place to wash your hands. All of this was nice, but so nasty. Every stool was either stopped up or had some sort of mess all over it. It was disgusting, so I waited until I went home and found a clean place.

The teacher we had was mean. If you didn't do your homework or something would tick her off, she would take a ruler and hit your palms about twenty times. One girl had lice and you could see them. She sent a note home to parents, telling them to get a fine tooth comb and get rid of the lice. So every day after supper we would get our heads scrapped. You could see the little white bugs on black paper.

We had about an eight mile ride to school on the bus everyday. Mr. Taylor was a good driver. This one school day we had a boy in our classroom that was so mean, someone told him that they wished he was dead. That day on the bus, Mr. Taylor stopped on the rise of the hill instead of the top. The little boy's sisters went across the road in front of the bus and the boy went across the road behind the bus. A tractor and trailer came over the hill and the little boy ran across the road in front of it. I looked out the window of the bus and there he was all mashed up. It made me sick to my stomach. We sat there for an hour waiting for help to come and pick the little boy up. When Mr. Taylor got back on the bus, he was a mess. I never forgot this. No one in our class ever wished someone would die again.

The fall went on and soon it was near Christmas. Dad bought two truck loads of slab wood from a lumber company. We borrowed a cut-off saw that ran on a belt from the pulley on the tractor. All that pile of wood had to be cut up. It took two people to carry a long piece and one to use the table, which pulled back and forth to cut the wood. My job was to pick up these heavy pieces and put them on the wood pile. It was a dangerous job because the saw had no shield. Luckily, no one got hurt and we had a winter supply of wood. We had corn cobs to start the fire in the morning along with lightning wood. On Sunday, that is what we would do in the fall and winter, when there were no chiggers or ticks. We would all get a grass bag and go back into the big wood to find a big old pine tree that had fallen down. Then we would get on top of it and walk the dead wood off of it. On the inside of the tree you would find lightning wood.

Our tractor went bad, so Daddy traded it off and got a newer Farm-all A. It was much better and easier to drive. Mama even talked Daddy into buying another cow. It was a big mistake; the new cow was a Jersey cow instead of a Guernsey cow. The cow wouldn't let anyone milk her. This made Daddy mad, so he took the truck and went to a dairy farm near Williamsburg. There he bought a calf and brought it home tied up in a grass-bag. He tied the Jersey cow to the manger before he brought in the other calf. The cow bellowed out and the calf got scared and went through the side of the barn. The Jersey cow came out of the stable with the manger tied around her neck. The calf took off for the big woods, scared to death. It took us two days to find the calf and return it home. It was quite a sight to behold.

Mama was having company for dinner. Daddy was gone and the two roosters had to be killed. She went out to the hen house and caught the roosters. She then tied their legs and started to chop off their heads on the stump where we split wood. She tried again and again, missing each time. She then asked me to kill them for her. I had never chopped off a chicken's head before; however, I took the axe and completed the task. From that point forward, I would cut the heads off of the chickens.

Daddy would take the 12 gauge shot gun and go squirrel hunting early in the morning. I loved squirrel with thick brown gravy and potatoes. So I talked him into teaching me how to hunt. I was almost eight years old and I could do many things––drive, milk cows and everything else on the farm. Since

I could do so many things, I might as well learn to hunt too. The shotgun would hurt your shoulder when it went off, so I would wear extra padding. In about three months, I became good at hunting.

Christmas was coming and we found a big tree to tie up in the corner again. We were all looking forward to Christmas this year, because Mama and Daddy went shopping. This Christmas, I got a bat and a real ball. Before this, I only had a makeshift ball made of twine and cloth and a bat made of spare boards. I loved to play ball, walk the barrels and ride hogs. We would play house in the summer by tying mare's tails together and cleaning the ground with them until it was smooth. We would make nice houses to play in.

Getting back to Mama needing chickens killed for company coming, after she had them picked, she called us into the house to clean the silverware. She put them into a dish pan and had us rub sand on them until they shined. We had received a letter from Aunt Ellie and Uncle Dan stating that they would be coming for dinner on Sunday. Aunt Ellie was Daddy's sister and she ran a boarding house in Newport News for men that worked at the shipyard. They had a two story house with six rooms that they rented. She would feed them a meal a day. We thought they were rich. They came to see us just to talk Daddy into driving them home to West Virginia.

Daddy agreed to take them home, but he decided to take Mama and the baby along. The catch was that I would be in charge of the farm for the week they were gone. My sister, who was married to a blind man named Ted, came to stay with us. All she liked to eat were stuffed green peppers. We hated them. I mean, absolutely HATED them. There was an old ham in the smoke house, so we cut slices of that and fried it with eggs. We also made hot biscuits, leaving my sister to eat all of those stuffed green peppers. I made out decently, taking care of the farm and going to school.

Daddy took on more than what he had bargained for by taking his sister and her husband home. During World War II, everything was rationed including tires for the car. They had ten flat tires going to West Virginia and eight coming back home. He was angry when he got home and didn't even thank me for doing a good job taking care of the farm while they were away. This I became accustomed to.

Spring returned and it was time to cut Irish potatoes, bed sweet potatoes, hot bed cabbage plants, and ready the land for planting. I was now eight and a half years old, so more responsibility was placed on my shoulders. My sister, Peter went to stay with Grandmother. Uncle Roy was in the Army and Uncle Clyde was crippled with arthritis. My Grandmother never had anything to do with us. She never came to see us, give us anything--she did nothing for us. Uncle Clyde was a mean uncle. Buggie and I loved to hunt for food to eat. We always had molasses buckets for picking berries. We found asparagus in the fence rows. In the middle of Grandma's cornfield was a tree with pretty red apples. They were all over the ground. Close to Grandma's house was a pear tree which had the best tasting little yellow pears. The corn was about ready to tassel and when no one could see us, we crawled on our knees to go get some of those pears and apples off of the ground.

We went up the lane and crawled down the cornfield. We filled our dresses up with the apples and pears. We then started down the cornrows home. At about the same time, shots rang out. Uncle Clyde yelled at us to get out of there, called us dirty little rats and told us to leave the apples behind. We dropped them and ran. He shot again.

We sprinted home; telling no one what had happened. From that point forward, we only looked for blackberries and huckleberries.

One day we wandered into the woods and found a new place. We found a big patch of huckleberries and blueberries. We had never found blueberries before. We filled our buckets full and went home. Mama made us dumplings for supper. Little did we know, those bushes with the blueberries were full of chiggers. We itched all over for a week. But we still went back to get more of them. We loved hunting for food. Our parents never knew where we were.

Daddy wanted to go fishing. He said he wanted some fresh fish, and we asked if we could go, too. It was a long way through the woods, to the pond. It was a big pond and we were not allowed to fish in it. It belonged to a fishing club in Richmond and if they caught you fishing there, they would put you in jail. We went fishing there anyways. We went down in the woods and found a small dogwood that would make a fine fishing pole. Then we cut the bark off of a big pine tree to use for corks. We used roofing nails for sinkers. With our box of hooks, we were ready to go fishing.

In order to find bait, Daddy took a bucket and a piece of wire. He made something like a crude crab net. We went into the swamp and found two deep holes. We pushed the wire under the tree roots and pulled up. There were crayfish in the wire. We put them into a bucket and started home to get our poles. We still needed worms, so we dug some up and placed them into a can. On the day that Daddy decided to go fishing, it had rained for three days straight. The fields were too wet to work in.

This was my first time fishing. Daddy said that it would be a long walk, so we hiked through the mud holes, and coated our feet with mud. Since we went barefooted, the mud protected our feet. We had our straw hats on, so the mayflies would not eat our heads up. In June, they were especially bad. We walked and walked, down the logging road. We found a path which winded through the trees until we reached the top of a long hill. We looked down and there was the water. Daddy checked things out so no one would see us fishing. I couldn't wait to put a worm on the hook and catch a fish. I had never even seen a fish before. I wondered what it would look like.

Daddy fixed our poles up, baited them, and showed us how to cast our lines out. After about three tries, my cork went under the water and I caught my first fish. It was a beautiful fish, a rainbow perch. We took him off of the hook and took a piece of twine through his mouth, tying him to a tree so he would stay in the water until we went home. I was excited. I caught more and more fish until we had a nice stringer of fish. Daddy caught a big bass. When we got home we cleaned them and had fish for supper. They were very tasty. I wanted to go fishing again the next day.

It was late June and time to dig Irish potatoes. We planted more this year, 14 acres of potatoes. It was hot in the afternoon, around three o'clock. We looked up and across the field, driving down Grandma's lane was a horse and buggy. The buggy and the horse were black. The man driving the buggy was dressed all in black. We all stopped and gawked at this sight. Daddy said "At least it's not coming to our house." Little did we know, Mama had gone to see Grandma. In a little while, she called for me and Buggie to come.

We unpinned our dresses and headed across the field. We wondered who the man on the buggy was. Mama made us come into the breezeway and sit on the stairs. The mean uncle was sitting near us, at the top of the stairs. In the hall were four rocking chairs. Grandma sat in one, Mama in another, and the man on the buggy sat right in front of us. He retrieved a book and began to carry on about something. Then he made us close our eyes and pray. I didn't even know what praying was. The man continued to talk at length. Uncle Clyde looked down at me and said, "Stick the old bastard, stick the bastard." I was using my safety pin to clean under my fingernails at the time. I didn't know what to do. Uncle Clyde continued to repeat himself. We thought it was funny and started to laugh. The man stopped praying and said some unkind words to Grandma and Mama. We got a beating like you would not believe when we returned to the potato field. I called this my first religious experience. My family never went to church or even saw a Bible. We didn't understand what the man in the buggy was doing.

An hour later, Uncle Clyde showed up near the fence row that was between our two houses. He was still laughing over the incident earlier in the day. He asked us to come near the fence, because he had something for us. We unpinned our dresses and watched as Uncle Clyde stirred up a hornet's nest that he had found the day before. We ran and they ate us up. Daddy told us to lie on the ground and keep still, so that they would go away. After being beaten and stung, we had a quite day.

World War II was still going on and the government told Daddy that he couldn't sell his potatoes. With the 14 acres of potatoes, we wondered what to do with them. Then he got a letter from the government stating that if he put them into a pile, they would pay for them. The government people came, measured the pile and poured purple dye all over them so that no one could eat or sell them. It was an astonishing waste.

Daddy decided that since we had so many cull potatoes and strings left from the sweet potatoes that he would raise more hogs. On the Tokarz farm, there was a nice barn with two sheds off on each side, so that he could put in pens for the sows to have their pigs there. We fenced in the land around the barn, a total of about ten acres. The fence went into the wood, near a nice stream. This way the sows and their pigs could have water and protection from the weather. Daddy ended up with 18 sows and a mean boar hog. There were wooden trays to feed the sows, and a fenced in area for the younger pigs to get their food.

This fenced in area would also be where the young pigs were castrated. Since

Daddy didn't know how to castrate pigs, he would ask Lin Burges to help him. All he would ask Daddy for after he performed the castrations were the mountain oysters and a bottle of whiskey.

Daddy was a drinker and when he started drinking he would not stop. The drinking upset Mama. When she learned that he brought home a bottle, she would ask my younger sister and I to find the bottle. She said that she would pay us ten cents, which was a lot of money. Off we went, searching everywhere. Finally, I found the bottle behind the toilet and I took it to her. She poured half the bottle out and put vinegar and hot peppers in it. She then shook the bottle and told us to put it back.

The next day came and Daddy did the chores. Then he told Mama that he was going to go see Mr. Oliver. Mr. Oliver loved to drink. We didn't know that he took the whiskey bottle with him. He offered Mr. Oliver a drink from the bottle. Mr. Oliver threw the bottle to his lips. The hot pepper was the first thing he tasted. Gasping, he cussed Daddy out and told him to never come back. Daddy came home and he was very mad. We hid in the barn and when we came home the table would no longer sit straight because of all the dents.

It was time to cat soybeans and we still had five acres of sweet potatoes to dig. Daddy decided that it was time to buy a combine. In a few days, we had a used one. I knew nothing about how to set the roller. Daddy was drinking and he told my sister and I to go to Roy's and cut his beans for him. We put the bags on the combine and Buggie rode the combine and I drove the tractor. We started cutting. There were about eight acres. It took us five hours to do. Unfortunately, we only had twenty bags of beans. Most of the beans spilled onto the ground. The dust was so bad, we didn't even check to see what we were doing. When Roy found out how many beans he had, he made Daddy pay him for what we had put on the ground. Everything seemed to be going wrong.

We finished digging sweet potatoes, just before the cold weather set in. They turned out well for us. Daddy went to see Mrs. Richardson and she agreed to let the electric company put poles across her field and the swamp to our house. Daddy bought Mama a gas stove and had a gas tank installed around the back of the house. The wood stove was gone and there was no heat in the kitchen. So, we got a tin heater. Mama could never get accustomed to that stove, but eventually she made out okay. They put electricity into our house just before Christmas. Daddy added onto the house and put on a living room with real furniture. We even had a bookcase with books.

For Christmas, he bought her a new bedroom suite and a crib for their eighth child. It was quite lovely. The dresser had a mirror, in which you could see a full-length view of yourself. The mirror had a glass shelf for you to keep your comb and mirrored brushes on. A couple of weeks went by and my sister Peter decided to look at herself in the mirror, just to see how pretty she was. Well the glass shelf broke. When I came in that evening from the tractor, Mama flew into me and Daddy gave me a beating. I told them that I hadn't been in the house all day and I didn't know who had broken the shelf. Peter started crying and said that she had done it. She apologized. That was the end of that. She said sorry and I got the beating for it. I think she was their favorite.

Christmas came again and I was nearly ten years old. I was getting quite tall, but I still didn't have any hair. The little bit that I had, I would wash it and take a paper bag to make rollers. You would tie your hair into strips of the paper bag and when you would wake up in the morning, you would have curls. Of course they didn't last long. By the time you walked down the lane to the bus, they were an event of the past. Oh well, at least I tried.

My sister Dick, her name is really Doris. She sent me a box of used clothes. There were two jackets, two skirts, a sweater, and two blouses. I now had store bought clothes. They were wonderful and made me feel almost pretty. It felt great not wearing feedbags.

We went hunting for our Christmas tree again. This year Mama bought us some tinsel and balls for the tree. It was quite pretty and we had decorated it well. I really wanted clothes this year. Christmas morning came and I had two pairs of jeans and a plaid shirt. They would keep me warm on the tractor and keep my knee from getting stiff.

It was time for Mama to have that baby now. Daddy took her to the hospital for this one. When he returned, he told us that Mama had another girl. Her name was Lucy, but we called her Dokie. Peter raised her, too; anything to keep out of the fields.

Moss Sherman had hogs, too. Well Daddy's male hog got out and went through Moss Sherman's fence. The hog killed all of Moss Sherman's male hogs. This started a little war, partially because they never liked each other anyways. He made Daddy pay for damages. It wasn't long after that, the same thing happened to him.

Moss Sherman needed a little help, so he came to Daddy and asked if he could hire my sister and I to turn his watermelon vines. Daddy agreed. We got up at 6 o'clock in the morning to eat our breakfast. We walked up the lane and back to the old house that was empty. It was a big field, about twelve acres. He was there with his tractor. He gave us two long sticks and showed us what he wanted us to do. We worked until one o'clock without a break. We had worked really hard. He knew we had tried, so he gave us a ride home in the back of the truck. When we got home, dinner was gone. Daddy was sitting under the pecan tree when we arrived. He had promised us fifty cents each for our work, but he didn't have any money to give us. He said he would pay us when he sold the tractor. He never did.

Summer was here again and Sundays were our day off from work. On this Sunday morning, I wanted to go fishing. I loved to fish and hunt. It was about 10 o'clock in the morning. The colored church's bells were ringing. They rang every Sunday. I dug up worms and we walked to the pond. We came to the top of the hill leading to the pond and the coast was clear, so we got our poles ready and baited our hooks. We cast our lines into the water. Suddenly, there were two men in a boat less than 100 feet from us. We dropped our poles and ran. They came after us, but we found a good place to hide under a dead tree. After they returned to their boat, we decided to head home. Well, we lost our way and even after we found our way back home, it was 1:30. Dinner was over with and we had two mad parents. I got a beating, but Buggie was spared because she told them that I had talked her into going. The next week Buggie got tick fever. She was in the hospital for two weeks and was close to dying. This is the second time any of us went to the hospital or doctor. Buggie lost all of her hair and went to live with Grandma.

Daddy decided that he needed a bigger tractor, so he went to McIntyre in West Point and they sold him a Super C Farmall Tractor. Instead of being red, it was white. The sun shining down on the hood would fix your eyes. He thought that he needed more land, too. So he rented another fifty acres at the Bradenham's farm, which was about eight miles away from home.

We now had 14 acres of peanuts, 16 acres of sweet potatoes, 12 acres of potatoes,

65 acres of soybeans and about 15 acres of corn. The potatoes had to be dug and planted by hand; the peanuts couldn't have grass or weeds in them. The corn had to be picked by hand and the beans couldn't have any weeds in them. Every thing had to be cultivated every week. Peter got married, Buggie lived at Grandma's house, Frog was too small to work, and Dokie was just a baby. That left me stuck at home. I would miss four weeks of school at a time. This happened all four years of high school. Daddy decided to plant ten acres of turnips. I pulled a truckload of them every evening to take to a Dairy farm on Route 5 near Williamsburg. They would grind them up

and feed them to the milk cows. The work became more and more.

I was voted into the Beta club when I was a freshman in high school. I got all A's and the occasional B. With the clothes that Doris sent me, I felt good about myself. I worked hard at home and at school. I was a good basketball player and loved baseball. I never could stay to practice, though. Because I didn't have a way to get home.

I needed something to drive on my own. While we were farming at Mr. Bradenham's farm that year, New Kent County was paying fifty cents for each ground hog's tail. There were plenty of ground hogs around. So Mr. Bradenham let me have 18 traps. He took the tails to the court house and gave me the money. It was 90 dollars. Mr. Higgs sold me a Model A Ford Car for $75.00. Now I could come and go as I pleased.

I wanted a horse of my own. Everyday on the school bus we would drive by Mr. Haley's farm and there was a big spotted horse that I wanted. I asked Daddy if he thought that Mr. Haley would let me take care of the horse. So we asked him and he said that I could take care of the horse. Daddy rode the horse home and I took the truck. This was the first time that he did anything for me. I had a beautiful horse now. I would go out riding every Sunday and I would do my homework on his back. I was so happy. I was now a Junior in High School with pretty used clothes, a horse, and a car. I thought I really had it good. I finally felt equal to everyone in my class.

School was good and I was able to come and go as I pleased. I was in the Beta club, safety patrol, on the baseball team, basketball team, and I could type. I was very proud of myself. But no one seemed to notice me. All the boys had girlfriends and all of the girls had boyfriends. They all knew that I was tough, though, and never messed with me.

In my junior year, I took a home economics class. It was a good class. One morning we made breakfast for the boys in the class. I made buttermilk biscuits, which I could make just like Mama did. The teacher, Mrs. Cowles, said that my biscuits were the best biscuits that she had ever eaten. She asked me for the recipe and I didn't even know what a recipe was. I told her that I just made them like I would at home and that I didn't have a recipe. So, she gave me a failing grade.

Then it came time to sew. I had been making my clothes since I was ten, but we never had a pattern. I would look at something, cut it out, and sew it up. Well, she wanted each of us to buy a piece of material, thread to match, and make something. We went to a store in Toano, picked out the pattern and the material. I found a pretty green corduroy and bought a skirt pattern. I cut it out, sewed everything together and it fit perfect. She told me that one of my darts was longer than the other one, so that I would have to do it again. I took it apart and it never looked right again. My skirt was not what I thought it should be.

Fall was a busy time. School was great but I had to stay home to help with the crops. The sweet potatoes were about half way done. We still had three more acres to dig. Then we would start on the corn. We had about 45 acres to pick by hand. Daddy hired three men to help him pull the corn and put it into the wagon. We had four big wagons. Mr. Bradenham would get one wagon and we would get three wagons of corn. We farmed on his place and he would get one fourth of whatever we farmed. This year we had thirty acres of corn and twenty acres of soybeans. This process would take two weeks, depending on the weather.

All of the machinery had to be greased everyday. We would buy a five gallon bucket of grease for the grease gun. Well, Daddy opened the bucket of grease and forgot that he left it near the barn. Bradenham had an old milk cow in the pasture. The cow found the bucket of grease and ate it all. That evening Daddy found the bucket empty. Mr. Bradenham found something else. He went to milk that cow that evening and every time she would turn around, she would mess on him. Fifteen feet away; everyway he turned, she would let him have it. That cow could not be gotten near for a week. She dried up and got as fat as a pig. That was the end of Mr. Bradenham's cow. Daddy had to buy him another cow and from that point onwards, he remembered where he left the grease bucket

In the afternoons, after we finished in the field, Daddy had to stop by Mr. Davis'. They would go down to the hen house and in a half of an hour, he would be drunk. When he got home, he would go straight to bed without supper, or milking cows, or anything. That meant that I had more work to do.

I got my driving permit at the age of 14. I was old enough to take charge now. The bags of soy beans had to be carried to Providence Forge to be weighed. The bags and strings would be brought home to use on the combine the next day. I would get up at 5 o'clock in the morning to be there at 6 o'clock when they opened. Most of the time I was second or third in line to be weighed. When I finished, I would go to school to drop off my homework and pick up my assignments for the next few days.

All of the crops were up by the middle of December. The corn bins were full, the hay barns were full, and the hogs were getting fat. The slab wood arrived and we borrowed the cross cut saw and cut up the pile of wood. We were ready for Christmas again. I really didn't want anything; I just wasn't in the mood. My sister sent me another box of clothes to wear. They were so nice.

Mary got married in the fall, and I forgot to tell you this. She was expecting a baby. She married my sister's husband's brother (the giant). Her new husband had quite a name. Let me tell you it: John Thomas Lorence Jenison Terrell III. I went to stay with her for a week and she gave me a beautiful skirt. It was green plaid and fit me just right. She had a little girl, who was born at home as well.

The winter passed and long hours on the tractor began again. I went fishing and hunting every chance that I had. This was my quiet time. The summer was hot and Daddy was drinking more now. He carried me down to Mr. Bradenham's farm with four cans of gasoline at six in the morning. He said that he would be back in a couple of hours. Late in the afternoon, he still hadn't returned. Mr. Bradenham realized that I hadn't had any lunch, so he brought me something to eat and drink. At four o'clock the truck arrived and daddy said that he was sick, so he was going to sit under the tree. I asked him about my lunch and he replied that he was sick. Sick––he wasn't sick, he was drunk. I took him home at five and all the chores still had to be done.

A week later, he decided to get Lin Burgess to castrate the pigs. After they finished, all

Burges wanted were the mountain oysters and a bottle of whiskey. Daddy took him to West Point for that. He stayed a long time that day, even though we had a lot to get done. At five o'clock, Daddy returned and his head was bleeding. He looked at me and said that it was all my fault––that I should have gone with him. I asked him where the truck was and he replied that it was up the lane and in the woods. I took the tractor with a chain up the lane. He had driven the truck right into a tree. The radiator and bumper were pushed right into the engine. Tying a chain to the back of the truck, I pulled it out into the road and towed it home. Daddy sobered up the next day and promised that he wouldn't do it again. It didn't happen again for a long time. Things got better.

School started. I decided that I wanted to be valedictorian of my class, so I had to take an extra class. My grades were all A's except for 1 B. I was now 16 years old. Our bus driver was coach of the boy's basketball and baseball teams. So he needed a school bus driver on the days that he couldn't drive. He knew I was a good truck driver, so he asked me if I would like to fill in for him. This meant that I would be making extra money, something I didn't have. We took the bus and went to Providence Forge to take the test; driving and written. Passing them both, the instructor told me that it was the first time that he gave a 16 year old girl a school bus license. My first day of driving by myself was bad. I was scared. The narrow road, and turning around was nerve-wracking. After a couple of times, it got better. I never asked my parents if I could do this. They never said anything about it.

It was October now, and we started to pick corn by hand. The wagons were ready. It was a Thursday and Daddy decided that he wanted something that would pick corn for him. He went off to McIntyre and bought a corn picker. He was driving along quite well when we got off the bus. Shirley was still living with Grandma and Betty and I headed home. I had to change clothes to start unloading the wagon. I thought that a corn-picker was a pretty good idea.

I had no sooner changed clothes when I heard someone howling. I realized that it was coming from the corn field up the lane. I got into the truck and drove there as fast as I could. Daddy was caught in the corn picker. His arm was all chewed up. The tractor was still running. I cut it off and grabbed wrenches from the tool box. He was sweating blood. His arm was smashed, so it was not bleeding badly. It took a little while to get the machine apart and get his arm out. He was getting weak. I got him into the truck and drove to Toano. Dr. Snead was still in his office and when I brought Daddy upstairs, he told me that there wasn't anything he could do. He said that I would have to take him to the hospital. He told me where to find the hospital in Williamsburg. I drove him to the hospital and the nurse told me that he would have to be signed in. She asked me if my mother was with me. I replied that she wasn't with us and the nurse told me to go home and get her.

I went home and explained to Mama what happened. I drove her back to Williamsburg. The preacher in Toano found out about what happened. He came to the hospital. He told me to go home and that he would bring Mama home. I drove home. I was tired and weak; it was 11:00 pm and the cows still had to be milked. I tried to eat something, but couldn't.

I got down on my knees in front of the window and prayed to God. I asked him to please help me. I didn't want to be on the farm for the rest of my life. The moon was full. I felt at peace and fell asleep. That was the first time I ever prayed. I heard that God answered prayers, so I put my trust in him.

The next day was Friday and I knew that I couldn't go to school. It just wouldn't be right. So I stayed home and worked on the farm. While I was working at the barn, two men showed up. One was young and really handsome, like you wouldn't believe. The other was a little older. They told me that they had heard about my father and had come from McIntyre to help get in the corn crop. We went up the lane in our trucks and I showed them the tractor and the picker. They put it back together and started picking corn. My sister and I took the other tractor and started cutting soybeans. By the end of the day, we had cut a load of soybeans to go to market and corn to be unloaded.

They really worked hard for us for the next few days. The following week, I stayed home from school, too. The teacher sent my homework home with my little sister.

The young man who helped us on the farm asked me for a date. I didn't even know his name, but I did like him. I accepted and we went out together. He made me feel special. It was a wonderful feeling to have someone really like you. I was really happy and couldn't wait to see him again.

Daddy came home from the hospital and was doing pretty well. His right arm had to be cut off. They decided it was time for a bathroom in the house and closed in the porch. Mr. Smiley came to close in the porch and put in a bathroom for us. We had to dig a hole for the waste to go and John went with me to Urbana to buy two loads of oyster shells to go in the drain field. I couldn't believe we had a bathroom. I had never taken a bath before--it felt so good, my body couldn't believe it.

Daddy still couldn't do anything, so most of the work fell to me. Mr. Hazelwood came and gave Daddy a $100.00 bill. He cried because he really needed it. The Dean men picked our corn and beans that year at Mr. Bradenham's farm. People were really nice to us. Christmas came and we put up a tree. John gave me a charm bracelet with my name on it. He picked me up and took me to meet his family. They hugged and kissed me. This had never happened to me before. We sat down at a beautiful table with silverware, candles, and china dishes. They said a prayer before the meal. They treated me like I couldn't believe. I thought that God must be answering my prayers and pouring his blessings on me. I promised him that I would change, now I knew why.

I did well in school that winter, getting all A's, driving the school bus, playing ball, and doing chores at home. Most of all, I enjoyed going on dates with John. He would write me a letter each week and we would go out on Saturday nights. July came and he asked me to marry him. I was in seventh heaven. No more farm. Thank you God. I was driving to Toano with Daddy in August to deliver a load of watermelon. He told me that if I didn't get married and stayed on the farm, that he would give me the farm. I thought that he had to be kidding. I loved John and he loved me.

November 30 came, it was a Sunday. This is the day we would be married. At 2:00 in the Parsonage in Saluda. John came and picked me up for our wedding. Mother, Dad, and my sister were sitting in the old living room.

We asked them if they wanted to come and they said no. I forgot to tell you about my Graduation in June. I was valedictorian of my class; and my family came to school for the first time to see me graduate. I was surprised. They gave Peter (Mary) a wedding, Buggie (Shirley) a wedding and three years of nursing school, and they gave me nothing. All of those years of hard work––nothing.

It wasn't long after we were married that Daddy got cancer. I went home once a week to see about them. We were talking and I asked Daddy, why we didn't have prayer at the table, or read the bible, or go to church.

He said, "Girl, I always say my prayers every night." "What a shame," I said, "we never heard you say a single one." And that was the end of that.

Eighteen years after Daddy died, we had to put Mother in a nursing home. It was a cold day in January, my birthday to be exact. I fixed a nice oyster dinner for her. I knew she loved oysters, so I brought her this dinner at the nursing home. I reminded her that it was my birthday. She said that she didn't have anything to give me. I replied that all I ever wanted her to do for me was to tell me that she loved me. She said, "I guess you're right." And that was the end of that. I left very disappointed, but I was happy because I had someone at home who really loved me.

We have three wonderful daughters who are all married. We have five grandchildren. Our daughters are Susan, Bonny, and Melinda. They have wonderful husbands––Brian, John, and Bill. We go to church every Sunday since we have been married. This year will be 56 wonderful years. With a husband as wonderful as John, I know my prayers have been answered every day that I am on this earth. We celebrated John's 75th birthday in September with 182 people present. I have Parkinson's and this is my 5th year with it. I am doing quite well with the love and prayers from my husband.

This is the story of what my life was like when I was growing up. I wanted to leave it to my children and grandchildren. Life is good if you love God and your family.

May God bless you, through me.

ABOUT THE AUTHOR

WHY I wrote the book BUNKIE. My husband was sick and in the hospital when I thought about writing a book on my childhood. We lived in a different world from what children live in now; so I thought I would tell about my world when I was little; so this is how BUNKIE got started.

1 was born at home; the fifth girl of eight. We lived in a poor house with no running water; no electricity; no phones; no books;

no bathroom; no, nothing that we are used to now. We were poor, but so was everyone else we thought, so it didn't matter at all.

We never went to a doctor, a dentist or church; but we all had to go to school and work in the fields at home. Parents had children to work the farm back when I came along; and that is what you had to do ... no ifs and ands about it either; that's how it was.

So, I learned early in life to make your own fun and be happy no matter what came along. I learned everything I could learn. I made it fun. It became a game to be better than anyone around me; so this was important to me. It made me strong, and I always stood-up for what was right. I learned later in life that life is not about me or things of this world; but life is a journey through this world into the next world of wonderful things that GOD has in store for us in Heaven. So, I made it my goal to help others that are in need, so it has become a blessing to me to be able to do this in GOD'S name; not mine.

All the money this book makes will go to a Rescue Mission to help children, mothers, fathers, the homeless; and chIldren to go to college or to school, or a trade school to learn to become something that they might like to be. This will be GOD helping me, to help Him. THIS is MY gift TO OTHERS. May you be blessed by my story; so my story may be a blessing to others.

GOD bless you, Love V. M. Brooke - BUNKIE

Printed in the United States
By Bookmasters